Ghosting

Poems
Steve McCown

D1066643

Up On Big Rock Poetry Series
SHIPWRECKT BOOKS PUBLISHING COMPANY

Minnesota

IN®
DIE

Cover & interior design by Shipwreckt Books

For Barbara Belobaba

Ghosting

The Only World We Knew

Pocketed

How much money I planned to steal
depended on how much was there:
a lot, more; a little, less.
Keep the math simple: add, subtract.
Don't awaken suspicion.

Yet, stealing from my mother's purse,
I was stolen in turn.
A tortoiseshell brush, ruby red lipstick
and Chanel No. 5
took my sixteen-year-old breath away.

So did the leather handbag's portable maze—
pockets within pockets,
compartments within compartments.
My fast fingers soon lost themselves.

A gold compact mirror
captured pieces of me,
blurry, distorted: an eye, a lip, a nose, an ear.

My father was there, too,
his photograph tucked in a buttery yellow wallet.
Clad in a herringbone tweed suit
at his college desk,
he eyed me, knowingly.

I often withdrew empty-handed,
yet her purse remained a soft, suede, redolent box.
Once opened, it released
the mysteries of her world.
Everything I touched touched me,
left its mark, print, scent.

Spit

"Come here, "my cousin breathed.
"I have something important to tell you."

Rumors?
Oracles?
Secrets from the other world?
I raised my head and listened.

To clarify her feelings
and keep them private,
she cupped her hands, cave-like, over my ear,
coughed and hacked and conjured up
her innermost saliva,
and then spit into my ear.

I was dripping, riddled with saliva.
Wetting my words, as if I don't
have enough of my own
to purge, to share,
I have been clearing my head ever since.

Fashion Statement

In my church's changing room
I could not find a fit.
Each Sunday I rifled through black acolyte robes
on high hangers attached to the doors,
rack after rack of vestments floated above me,
the arms, the backs, the shoulders
eluding mine, eluding my sizes.
The robes were too big or small,
nothing in between,
nothing tailored to fit.

My blue jeans, my red tennis shoes,
were loud like statements,
while the worn darkness, falling
and falling, spreading out,
covered me in its long, swishing, dragging night.

War Games

The American Revolution
lasted ten minutes,
the Civil War twenty,
World Wars I and II,
an hour.

Marshaling our soldiers in rows,
we fought epic battles
on plush carpet,
barked orders, uttered screams,
yells, taunts.

We mixed up men,
created new wars:
GI Joes shot Confederate soldiers,
Union soldiers blasted Red Coats.

Each side won, each side lost.
Suffering battle fatigue,
we stashed history away,
every armed piece,
in boxes, saved until tomorrow,
another bloody day, repeated
in joy again and again.

House Painter

At the foot of a ladder leaning against a bare wall,
he rested sideways
on spotted ground, in the shade of a paint- scraped house,
fumes escaping from open pots.

Rumpled hat, baggy pants,
and round, fat stomach—
 a drooping snowman.

His white clothing
was streaked blue,
stippled red and pink, stained grey.
Uncovered roses, daises,
dribbled on, smeared,
a toxic motley.

His coarse whiskers stood out stiffly,
a black growth. He was eating,
gazing at us. He offered us bright candy
in exchange for rubbing cheeks,
his on ours.

We accepted,
too young to know
how slippery candy can be
when swallowed whole.

Stolen Jesus Sips

I am the True Vine (John 15:1)

Every Sunday, by the time I received Communion,
I had already taken it repeatedly.
An acolyte with a key to the wine cabinet,
I had a taste for liquid symbolism.

But my tongue proved confessional at heart,
purpling, reddening;
grape skins colored the telltale surface.
Around the pastor I kept it locked inside.

Speaking was dangerous,
and so was singing, reciting.
Even breathing was risky.
I mumbled tight-lipped prayers,
afraid the spirits might escape.
I spoke to myself
in strange tongues.

In night dreams,
my tongue hung out,
lolling, dripping, panting
wildly in Christ's Vineyard.

Delivered

A white Victorian mansion faced me,
surely haunted,
home of the bishops,
and luxurious lawns only starlight
was allowed to play on.

The other lights were a push button doorbell,
an angelic fingerprint,
and a dormer window
hoarding office light inside
a small attic.

The doorbell unlocked the door.
Four floors.
I felt my way up
a splintery banister,
counted steps,
and jiggled my change pouch,
tallied up sums
in my head
for newspapers delivered,
abandoned in shadows.

I knocked. The door opened,
a hand gave me money,
exact change, then
closed the door
on stark fluorescence.

Collecting myself,
I felt my way down
and out, relieved
to see starlight
dancing on dark grass.

Rungs

My grandmother wrote me into her house
on a kitchen doorframe,
my lettered place as prominent
as her oak table and carnival glassware.

Each time I visited she marked my height,
signed my name next to the line,
and dated the entry on painted wood.
To this living chronicle—substantial
as a totem pole or column of Chinese characters—
she inscribed words of encouragement
running onto the adjoining wall:
"great progress," "keep growing," "fantastic."

I could never grow fast enough.
My back against the frame,
straining and stretching,
I rose to her ruler and pencil,
to the rungs of her writing
on which I had hoped to climb forever.

When the words ceased, a white space
appeared above my name,
extending to the ceiling and beyond,
to the other tidier house where
my height, my growth, my yearnings,
on their own,
went unmarked.

A Tractor on the North Shore near Lake Superior

Abandoned in birches, a farm tractor,
rusty and mossy, without a field,
dead in its ferny tracks, transported me.

Every morning on a cabin-crowded vacation,
near a craggy shoreline in fog-bound silence,
I fired it up, gave the old thing sound.

Articulating parts, mimicking pistons,
voicing silent cylinders, I ran it
at full throat, speaking for both of us.

We went nowhere, we went everywhere.

For Our Ears Only

Leaving the green field,
abandoning bikes, gloves, and parents,
but still in uniform,
we Junior League stars celebrated our victory
in a nearby empty band shell.

Hidden yet on display,
we scraped a chorus of cleats on risers,
spiked stolen beer cans open,
a spitting crescendo,
and with our fingers snapped tabs
like castanets—

sweet music only we enjoyed
on a summer night.

Miry Ascent

Inspired by W.H. Auden's "Musee des Beaux Arts"

No waxy Icarus—sun-blinded, sun-singed—
I fell into a dumpster once,
backwards, grabbing whatever I could
on my short flight: handles, rust, air.

Plummeting into the depths,
I rummaged for my glasses
thrown out with the trash,
my vision lost in an underworld,

the lenses glinting up at me
from the bottom of a portable abyss
with greasy blackened walls.

I waded in ooze.
I stepped in liquefied meat,
inhaled the belly of the beast.

When I rose again,
red marks, coffee grounds,
and lettuce leaves like crumpled
wings covered my shoulders.

Ring Spinners

1.
Tight, idle silver on our fingers,
we yanked our class rings free,
spun them on desktops,
cafeteria tables,

and they danced over cracks and carvings,
pirouetted on stains,
and circled each other ecstatically—
small dervishes near the edges.

2.
In time we perfected our spinning skills,
learned to balance rings
on their poles. A tip of a finger,
pressed down just so,

stopped sapphire,
arrested the year (1969)
and halted the engraved logo hawk
from flying off the surfaces

of the only world we knew.

Swimming Lesson

Black on blue,
the inner tube taken from a tractor tire
churned in the pool's shallow end,
spun by kicking kids
straddling it.

Outsiders on slippery tiles,
pool side, dive bombed the crowded raft.
Submerged subversives heaved the craft over.

Once, late to the rubbery merry-go-round
and trying to land a place,
I jumped, slipped on the surface
and plunged through the hole,
flushing myself into a red-eye panic.

Thrashing feet, oblivious, knocked me under
when I struggled to ascend.
Again and again I struck my head
against a soft ceiling,
a bloated, circular centipede.

Slowly I sunk
beneath a black cloud
storming with children
screaming above my muted world—

until I swam free, found room,
movement, air, and breath in the deep end.

Dirty Laundry

Even then I relished sound,
dropping tennis shoes down a laundry chute.
A whoosh, a thud rose up to me,
and an enlivening backlash
of tunneled wind.

I tipped a dictionary into the abyss.
The weight of words
banged and echoed against the tin shaft,
the definitions resonating
in the vertical chamber,
a belly-flat climatic plunk at the bottom.

I dropped my voices as well:
a whisper, a yell, a scream.
High in my parents' home, I spoke
through three floors into the basement,
to the basement—an underworld
I feared, placated with speech,
frightened with sheer noise.

Unaware I was listening
(I was unaware it could speak)
the subterranean spoke once:
Claire, our laundry woman, alone,
hot iron in hand, ranting to herself,
sweating and swearing over my shirts,
my sheets, my towels, my pants.

A Baseball Card

1.
We bit through the plastic wrappers,
then tore them open with our teeth.
Forced entry into Olympus:
five baseball heroes per packet
and a stick of bubble gum.

Mays, Mantle, Spahn,
Clemente and Cepada
were framed on individual cards.
On one side, pictures;
on the other, statistics.
We studied our math first
and then savored the gum
greatness had touched.

I once licked the sugary residue,
the pink powder,
from Hank Aaron's smiling, delicious face.
A friend, gumming his words,
muttered, "You just kissed a nigger."

2.
We put our heroes to the wheel.
Clothespins fixed the baseball cards
to bicycle spokes.
A winged ruckus, a wild, flapping sound,
staccato-like the faster we pedaled,
our icons slapped silly at any speed—
we thought we could fly with them.

Some cards flew off in time,
never seen again. Others were shredded.
Boys of summer once, a few stubborn veterans,
weathering our cycling seasons,

clung to the bars in tatters or caught
in the wheels, throwing off our balance
as we veered into dreams.

Otherland

After the storm, we walked in trees,
on the backs of old elms
tossed over our playground like pick-up sticks.

In a line we balanced on a hundred exposed rings,
crossed to another hundred,
then branched out, slowly, to the ends:

a leafy mass shrouding a swing set,
a cluster of unearthed roots
stopping a merry-go-round forever, in mid spin.

Split in two, a teeter totter
lost its equilibrium.
A jungle Jim was smashed,

our monkey motions banished.
Yet we explored the wreckage.
One playground replaced another.

The toppled, the crushed, led us up
to the highest limbs, to the fallen heights.

A Team of One

The hitter slammed the ball,
glanced heavenward,
then flung his bat behind himself.
The fans erupted in a roar.
I scampered after it.

In the on-deck circle, bat and bat boy
collided, the barrel end bludgeoning my shin
as the ball soared over the right field fence.

The slugger floated over the bases.
No one saw the collision.
I didn't want anyone to see.
My uniform, from the knee down,
changed colors, changed teams,

and suddenly, I was a team of one.
I was everywhere, nowhere, at once.
Diamond and dugout and resin bag vanished.

Placeless pain, transcendent, sent me reeling
above the rainbow-arcing homerun ball
that for many adoring fans of the star
would never land.

The Glue Sniffers

We heard them first,
like bellows slowly worked,
fanning dying embers

or iron lungs
compressing and expelling
regulated air.

A music of sorts
they made, a doomed duet—
two microphones left on in the dark,

amplifying stifled background sounds.
Then we saw them:
their breathing brought life

to paper, the brown grocery bags
caving in over their mouths,
then wrinkling out slowly,

the sides and tops quivering like cauls.
Their covered heads were
hidden in contained clouds,
the fumes of glue swirling
with each breath
like waves collapsing on themselves.

They sat side by side
against our school,
their legs sticking out straight as planks.

A near perfect tableau:
nothing moved except paper,
nothing heard save bagged breath,
nothing seen except eyeless masks.

Eleven and twelve and thirteen,
we held our breath
all the way home.

Shadowy Exits

Yuma Territorial Prison
Yuma, Arizona

1.
Their words,
are still imprisoned,
scratched into walls,
dug into iron bed frames.
Almost illegible:
life in a cell.

2.
When the prison closed,
a temporary school opened here.
Students trudged in bearing belt-strapped books
slung over their shoulders,
and stared for years at the walls.

3.
Hard times locked in;
iron rails led many to these unlocked cells.
The dispossessed, the displaced, wrote the most:
dates carved into stone; family names gouged out.
"headed east, headed west
lovely quarters."
"The Robinsons: Mary, Martha, Jane,
Bill, Greg, David, Ann."
"Here for a night, gone soon,
Speakly Weeks 1934"

4.
An inland armory and watchtower:
The Japanese are invading!
The walls are ramparts,
and internment camps spring up,
slapped together in the deserts.
Elsewhere, names are numbers in skin,
and history dropping from the sky,

or rising like a gas in crowded cells.

5.
The prison stolen,
brick by adobe brick,
iron grates, medieval-like doors,
bars, flagstones—building materials,
home improvements, city renewal.
What remains are the remains.

6.
We stroll the yard, skim old news articles,
glance at mug shots and peek into cells.
We leave in no time.

Body Parts
Induction Physical—1970
Minneapolis, Minnesota

I stuck to the yellow stripe,
followed it through narrow Federal corridors,
upstairs, down.

My directed senses found their offices:
eyes to the ophthalmologist,
ears to the audiologist.

I was divided.
I couldn't see, I couldn't hear,
I failed everything.

A cold stethoscope listened
to my snare drum heart.
An arm wrap pressured me, tighter and tighter.

A tiny upstart hammer knocked my knees.
A flashlight squeezed in the grip of policy
stared blindly into my vacant eyes.

I dropped my towel,
white as the cracked walls,
and bent and reached and touched my toes.

I held my position
so trained eyes above could exam what I couldn't—
exclusive information.

I hopped one-footed in place,
a pogo stick in a circle
of other jumping sticks.
The ragged ring exhausted itself.

My probed gums, examined teeth

and tongue were healthy for now.

Blood drawn out was blood lost.
The war was lost.

Badlands

A few years after the famous battle
you didn't have to dig deep
to strike history like gold.

Hard objects survived
below rabbit brush and snakeweed:
arrowheads, spent cartridges,
lance tips, a bone here, there.

No shortage of those artifacts,
and collectors unearthed Colt revolvers,
epaulettes, beaded quivers.
No laws preserving the site,
you could scavenge at will—
a thief's field day.

From the Montana Badlands
many souvenir hunters
brought home
in deep pockets, in bags,
for inventory and sale
the material remains
of the 7th Calvary and Lakota Sioux.

A Touch of War

From the class discussion he turned abruptly
and faced me with a face of war.
It wasn't what I expected,
wasn't mangled, radically rearranged, Picasso-like.
Nor did it evoke burning villages
from which naked children,
also burning, ran screaming
to other villages aflame.

Yet he leaned closer:
a moonscape of thin, white lines,
crisscrossing themselves continuously,
emerged slowly through
the smoky haze of his beard.

Shrapnel. Flying from a near bomb,
it took cover in his face,
hid under his skin for years
numerous and minute—
the burning bits, the slicing slivers—
to be extracted without "causing deeper damage,"
he stated, laughing ironically.

"Touch here," he ordered, and I did.
My fingertips were green recruits
traversing a pebbly path
twisting from chin to temple.

"And here." A multitude of edges,
like scrap metal in a junkyard,
jutted from his scalp.

"And all across here." His fingers guided mine
over scars like white, petrified worms.
Beneath them was a loose mosaic,
whose pieces are never missing,

whose picture is clear to no one.
A mask unseen, it asserted its design
privately, fragment by fragment, every time
he smiled, grimaced, laughed, frowned.

"You can't see it, but I can feel it always."
His face was Braille—across an unfathomable space
between us I reached
and read it as deeply as I could.
Then, closing old textbooks, we talked.

Fallout—1961

Marshalling us into a strict line,
our teacher led us down,
from classroom to fallout shelter,
school to subterranean school,
The Cold War waiting in the basement.

Saved from textbooks,
we whispered goodbye to civics,
history, the principal's office,
relieved to practice evacuation drills
instead of division and fractions,
or to assemble plastic atom models
and disassemble them.

Yet not relieved; the sooty walls
didn't seem strong enough.
We inhaled dust, liquid cleaning fumes,
and remembered our janitor
once opening a winter furnace too soon,
blasting his brows, hair, and skin
to kingdom come.
Survived diminished.

Half shadows, we grew antsy in the twilight,
squashed spiders, examined
an ancient system of dripping pipes,
imagined relatives above, on ground zero.
Three kids began to cry.
The other curriculum took hold.
Giant clouds mushroomed in our heads.

Speaking in Codes
Navajo Code Talker Alfred K. Newman (1924-2019)

Your homework one school night:
write "I will not speak Navajo" five hundred times.
Forced to swallow the First Amendment
in class, you didn't choke,
but kept it breathing inside,
a deep allegiance, unbreakable.

Your assignment in Iwo Jima,
Guadalcanal, Peleliu, Tarawa:
speak Navajo code
to transmit a thousand radio and telephone messages.
No military terms in your Native tongue,
but tropes work,
life and death in figures of speech.

Tanks were turtles;
small boats, mosquitoes;
battleships, whales;
submarines, iron fish;
aircraft, bird carriers.

"Mobilize two turtles."
"Free three mosquitoes."
"Launch a whale."
Now your student,
metaphor-minded,
I imitate, memorialize.
Let iron fish swim,
bird carriers fly.

LO-TSO
BESH-LO
TISIDI-MOFFA- YE-HI

The Japanese couldn't crack your code,

nor could your Indian boarding school—
the vow of silence officially peeled
from your lips, declassified, in 1968.
Your warriors, public words, known now.
Have a good journey.

Nizhonigo cha'aanidinaal.

Thrones

Advice to a young king on the eve of his coronation

Heed this, your Highness:
straight-backed and rigid,
with a painful bas-relief design,
a throne is not made to be comfortable.

It is a cramped, three-sided office for one,
vulnerable in front. If my Lord brings a pillow
or rump cushion,
The Privy Council could toss it out
(unauthorized props, unkingly)
or pull the lofty chair from beneath your royal derriere.

If the throne is gold, you can't see the precious stuff.
How can you see what you are squatting on?
Your Highness will discern a duplicitous simulation
of gold, however, in the eyes of footstools
when they are allowed to gaze up at your crowned head.
But if their shining reflections blind my Lord,
you will not see the sun rising
and sinking on your kingdom.

Should that happen, you, my Sovereign,
can't pocket all that gold,
unless it is dismantled, melted,
in which case you lose your balance,
and the gold will pocket you.

Anger

Housing Project, 1972

There, to live in an apartment
was to live in others,
the walls skin-thin, in need of bones
and filler—plastered, unpainted
skeletons between families.

Everything heard.
So when I kicked up at the poor wall,
at the hollowness, blaring music,
fights and lovemaking, I crashed
through—between a warped mirror
and an unframed picture on my side,
and unseen wall hangings next door,
clattering down.

My dark sole faced neighbors.
One foot stood in my home,
the other stuck out in theirs—
a contorted Colossus of anger
straddling space and wreckage.

Lacerations

1.
From a Mississippi sandbar
I jumped on iron,
the river's tooth
waiting in welcoming water,
the tip of a submerged structure
history abandoned, washed over,
smoothed out on top
so I could not detect the spike below.

2.
Defying signs and fences,
I once ventured into a Marine base,
searching for desert wildflowers,
only to threaten tank bombs
left unexploded in sacred sand.
Dark pistols jiggling, an incendiary soldier
who tracked and saved me
from a dishonorable death,
screamed, "General Patton practiced here!
Have you no respect? Bombs are everywhere!
Get out now!" What could I say?
The pursuit of beauty blurs boundaries?

3.
Rushing to ply my hooks in the Iron River,
I dropped my tackle box, and lures
sprang out like tangled jewelry or robot innards,
including a three-pronged Daredevil
discovered missing when I inventoried
my compartmentalized barbs that night.
Often I think of a wading child,
or a dog, a wolf, a moose bending
to drink fresh Wisconsin water
with a metallic glint.

4.
Blood bubbled up from my lanced foot,
merged with other red tributaries
in a grand waterway
flowing gently, peacefully,
over our iron works.

Criminal

Fate feels like this,
metallic, too tight, blood cut off,
inescapable.

Cuffed by border agents,
iron-fisted men,
bound to their work,
I was coerced from car
to holding tank, processed.

My image and numbers ran
scared through a system
out of sight, out of reach.

Hands webbed behind my back,
fingers touched, clasped.
My armless chest stuck out,
a constrained masculinity,
forced bravado.

Trial by computer proved my innocence.
Unshackled, oxbow removed.
Freedom—a tiny key in a tiny hole.

In lieu of apology,
explanation, soft evidence
handed over, face up,
on an unreadable palm—

a picture of a killer
who looked like me
who wasn't me.

Mirrors
cast doubt—he stares at me,
free, still at large.

Opening and Closing
At Miller's bar in St. Paul, now closed

It sounded like a door opening and closing
against an object,
muffled somewhat in the women's restroom,
where Jimmy the bartender had followed
his wife as if he used both
whenever he felt a need.

The howling juke box,
cranked up even more,
chased away the screams.
We leaned back into the oblivion
of a pounding song.

Frozen on stools,
we cursed our clenched jaws,
brooded,
stared into open, mirrored rooms.

She exited first,
her face opened and closed.
Then out strode Jimmy,
going straight
to work behind the bar,
tidying up,
scrubbing mugs
and twisting a bar rag
(two red fingers tamping it down)
into the socket of a shot glass.

Men's Room

At a Greyhound Bus Depot
two poets stand side by side at the urinals,
rigid as fence posts.
Between them is a partial divider.
Rusty chrome fixtures blur and distort
their reflected faces.

Each knows the other's picture and poems,
but they have never met until now—
only now they haven't anything to say
to each other out of embarrassment,
and eyes up, nothing to see except a white-tiled wall
scribbled with graffiti: "Bill stood here."
"For a good time call 645-3211."

Trapped

Black, billowing, masked,
my Halloween costume
haunted me.

I made it extra-large,
roomy enough
for another self
I never knew existed

until I felt its breath,
much like mine,
quick, short;

shared eyeholes,
slits eclipsing sight;
uttered sounds
only we could hear.

In the stitched darkness,
together, we scratched at
seams sewn perfectly.

In this Flat World

Crossing the Line

Van Gogh Institute, Amsterdam

To look into his picture is to be in it,
to stand on red tiles, feel
a spring wash of blues and greens, repose
in a still life, every object at hand:
chair, pitcher, table, mirror.

And so I entered his *Bedroom In Arles*,
drawn by wall pictures within the picture
and by a glowing red blanket
on a yellow-orange bed,
the bulging ruby heart
half-hidden behind a massive footboard.

I wanted to touch red,
to see if the paint was built up,
rounded with a mysterious inner life
as if the artist had just risen,
left something vital for us.

And so my hand crossed the infra-red line
eyed sleepily by the museum attendant,
who mastered his *ennui*
to pull me out of the bedroom,
my eviction abrupt,
my imagination guilty of breaking and entering.

Hungry
Mexicali

In this border town
on a Sunday morning,
barefoot kids hawk curios:
yard ornaments,
cheap silverware,
placemats, plastic table flowers.

Car to car,
the scrawny peddlers work the traffic,
backed-up for miles in the sunlit dust.

Idling forward,
vacationing south
past children and trinkets,
I shut windows,
turn the radio up,
blast the air conditioner.

I stop; a boy in a ragged t-shirt
blocks my progress.
Above my hood ornament
and his head,
he hoists a decorative fork and spoon,
a matching set—dark stained,
long handled, carved
from gnarled wood,
and two or three times their normal size.

Too American

In a Parisian rain, at midnight,
I wandered through an arched entranceway
at the Sorbonne—two gendarmes
halted me in the courtyard.
In tipsy English and botched French,
I told them I was going to class.

At the Rijksmuseum,
I snap flashed Rembrandt's *The Night Watch*,
providing a light
to an aging, dark background
and to his colorful militia
which I wanted to join—
and then I posed for pictures in a security office
I'm part of their collection!

I crossed an infra-red line
at the Van Gogh Institute,
reached out and almost touched genius,
but was grabbed by a guard instead.

At Westminster Abbey I was told
to remove my Twins baseball cap
by a stern priest standing next
to a sculpted king on a crypt.
I wanted to lie down with royalty.

I hid in Anne's annex,
to get the feel of it,
but lingered too long
at her bulletin board,
gazing at pictures of old European movie stars
and reading Rodin quotes.
Soon, I was found,
forced into a long, long exiting line.

I jumped from a tour boat in Bruges,
too crowded, and lit out in the water.
From a tiny cup I downed twelve espressos,
paced around Luxembourg for two days.
Searching for gold and jewels,
I trailed a hooded priest
to Norte Dame's reliquaries
in subterranean vaults.

I read *Huckleberry Finn* in Bath,
in Jane Austin's house.
I kissed *Mona Lisa*,
tried to nestle into the marble lap
of *Madonna of Bruges with Child*—
not enough room.

Po'boy
New Orleans, Lafayette Cemetery

From a distance
we thought he was charging admission,
a young black Charon
outside the City of the Dead.

No money in our mouths
(so far as we could reckon)
as price of passage.
No coins weighing down tongues,
deadening, silencing them—
we could still taste, speak, and feel.

Skinny, back against a crumbling wall,
he wasn't taxing poor souls
but hawking sandwiches,
his livelihood next to him,
an open red cooler rich with Cajun spices,
battered shrimp, fried oysters, alligator—
a treasure trove of scents rising
like spirits, transporting us
in passing.

We toured the City.
All afternoon amidst marble and granite
we heard him shouting over
decaying mausoleums, once ritzy crypts,
and the wealthy dead,
"Po'boys, po'boys, po'boys"
for the life of him.

Guided by our noses and ears—
taste buds enlivened, mouths
watering, appetite deepened—
we emerged from the underworld
famished, and ate our fill.

Commerce

New Orleans

Tall, elegant windows
stand shuttered,
then as now,
in the Creole mansions
facing Esplanade Avenue,
where under sprawling oaks
chained slaves were "penned,
showcased and auctioned."

Old pillars, newly painted,
still bear the silent weight
of those who once lived above.

The live oaks tell more.
Limbs grow horizontally,
twist and bend to leafless ends.
Like fractured bones,
exposed roots enmesh our feet.
We stumble, clutching
at ropes of Spanish moss
hanging from the trees.

Tourists, we don't stay long,
walk to the next site
in the guidebook,
but for a tongue-tied moment
we are bound
to distant clanks and bids.

Yard Man
New Orleans

Jefferson Davis's mansion is closed today,
but not for the black yard man
masked in a white respirator,
working behind a wrought iron fence
topped with spikes, and hung
with a slanted historical sign.

Half hidden by the words and lances,
in front of old pillars
sunk deep, he plods on,
mowing and bagging acres of irony.

Conversion

Rosary beads clacking against the mirror,
Our Lady of Guadalupe pictures
trembling on the dash,
saints in niches leaning this way,
that way, the dented cab
a speeding shrine,
the driver hell-bent on hairpin turns,
sudden stops, sudden accelerations,
and a horn-blasting impatience
as if he were proclaiming
the Messiah's Second Coming
in Tijuana.

And in the back seat,
struggling to sit up straight,
I, a sinner, found Jesus for the ride.

Sundialed

In this park in Phoenix you stride out
onto an enormous sundial like a circular stage,
and gravitate toward the center,
to the current month; numbers, signs,
and symbols revolve around your body
as the sun and you tell time.
Cosmic systems love you.

You hate sunset,
want to stay here forever,
marking the hour
and inhabiting the Zodiac,
while you stand still,
the center of everything for once,
your shadow making the rounds.

Picture Day
Puerto Vallarta

Above and below us,
along the banks of the Cuale,
and in it, women work,
balancing laundry baskets
on their heads like giant crowns,
wringing from pants
the cold mountain river,
and pounding shirts against boulders
the size and shape of bending women.

We wade in their wash,
holding cameras high,
conscious of water spots,
sun glare, the right angles, focus—

and followed by a school of dim fish.

The Rope
Puerto Vallarta

The iconic, crowned church is closed.
The bell rope idles down
over still saints
behind darkened windows.

No one is near to pick up the end,
looped on the ground,
save a small girl,
all eyes, frayed dress, bare feet.
Her family is encamped tonight
against the holy walls.

Tempted, she lifts the rope gently,
as if it is silk
instead of a coarse braid,
a stray strand someone
forgot to put up.
Pulling it tight to test
the limits of her movements,
she plays, then pushes off ...

But how far can she go,
swinging out on the purest sound,
riding bells and sounding kingdoms,
and then flying back, screaming,
to her family against the wall?

Fate and Faith

Stopped, stuck in place,
we open eyes wide,
yet operate on blind faith.

Roaring into a city intersection,
a semi-truck turns and turns
inches from us, a circling
grey wall on wheels—

too close to read,
the bumper- to- bumper
black letters facing us,
and the cloistered driver unseen,
the engine firing like dragon's breath

as we hold ours and wait.

Table Land

Among many highway signs
one stands out,
a rust red invitation
to stop: Roadside Table One Mile.

Cement-made, massive, even monolithic—
for speeders turned picnickers—
the table resembles a stone altar without offerings.
Every time I travel this way
it is vacant, yet stolidly and improbably here,
waiting …

Nothing defines the table except itself,
fields and fields of space,
a few scrub bushes,
and whatever you set out and serve
in this flat world.

Crossing the Border

Noses on long leashes surround your car,
circle it, then vanish underneath
and reemerge without answers,
but still sniffing for contraband.

In a glass booth an armed guard puffs out his chest.
Between countries, he is his own country.
Leaning down, he questions your visible world
(car, registration, license, passport)
and the invisible one
(reason, purpose, ultimate destination).

Guns? Drugs? Citizen? Country?
He repeats each question in case you didn't hear.
You want him to believe your answers,
but, suddenly, you don't recognize yourself
in your own responses.

Suddenly, you are aware of pointed guns,
oil rags in the opened trunk,
dusty luggage dumped in a pile,
candy wrappers under the rifled seats,
cigarette butts in a sifted ashtray.

Through a dirty window you see what lies ahead:
border war casualties.
Justice and truth are the first to go,
double-crossed.
No flowers, no Crucifixes,
mark their graves
on either side.

Writer in the Northfield Library Restroom

An automatic hand towel dispenser,
touchy thing
without being touched,
scrolls sheets down
the moment I walk in
even before I have used the facilities,
before I have thought of anything.
My mere physical presence
triggers paper.

The God's Servant in the Fountain
Kansas City, Missouri

Below Neptune
the city worker slogs,
emptying the fountain.
Water swirls, drains,
around his waders
and this chariot-driving deity,
revealing a slippery mass of
dimes, nickels, pennies.

Caught in the vortex,
floundering in turbulence,
he is almost washed over,
his footing uncertain
below a rigid figure with iron eyes.

Wishes give way beneath his weight,
but he rights himself, maintains his balance.
He collects coins for his labors. To a god
and his charging steed, he hauls
buckets, brooms, brushes, garden hoses.

Basin empty, swept, mopped,
he now scales steel and scours the god—
the stained trident, the grimy beard—
and then fills up Neptune's sea again.

Water Music

Temperance River, Schroeder, Minnesota

As I crossed it, the bridge appeared to give way
to the sound of the river below,
so it seemed I was walking on a roaring,
a deep gorge swirling crashing,
the white foam crescendo—continuous,
substantial – holding me in midair,
like a poem whose strong cadences
leave you in awe, transfixed
on the structure of sound.

Seeing
Grand Marais, Minnesota

A rising dervish of birds
tricks the eye
into an airy illusion:
downtown is uptown here.

So many seagulls fly from the roofs at once
the buildings seem to follow them,
levitate a moment
under ascending wings, then
break free from their foundations
into hundreds of white pieces.

Everything light and heavy,
stationary and mobile,
returns in time to the same places:
a solid flock, building after feathery building.

Magritte defied gravity,
painted a boulder in midair,
topped with a tiny castle,
and he transformed a mountain range
into rocky wings——-
an immense eagle rising,
snowy head face up.

Our sidewalk vision,
accustomed to cracks,
takes flight as well,
lands when seagulls land
at the top of things.

Still Life
Grand Marais, Minnesota

No wind. No waves. No people.
Not a sail aflutter, a bow rising.
The rockbound blue water inert,
even reflections anchored,
three seagulls mute, mesmerized,
the harbor a perfect still life
into which I, new to the shore,
cast stones.

An Awakening
Dublin, Ireland

No cockcrow, no alarm clock
set to shout, no unfiltered blast of light—
just a slow drumbeat
penetrating our covers, nudging us.

More drumbeats,
one at a time,
with spaced intervals for reflection,
each beat punctuating the silence.
Consciousness becomes dramatic.
Our hearts stir.

We rise to street actors outside,
in ferocious black and white paint,
exotic costumes—
back-to-back Samurais,
almost a single figure,
Janus-like, standing outside
The Garden of Remembrance.

One warrior holds a drum,
the other a sheaf of programs.
Only their hands move,
bodies stoically still,
a tableau of flamboyant restraint.

The steady sound, summoning everyone,
is a call to art,
to Yeats' *The Dreaming Bones*,
a Japanese No play tonight,

to which we, fully awake now,
proclaim "Yes"
in the eerie Dublin light.

A Cindery Stage

On Visiting an Ex-Drama Student
in Jail

The yellow brick road
you starred on
ends here:
in a six by eight-foot cell.
I won't lecture you.
You are beyond that now.
Nor will I say that jail time
is like class time as others have said.
In these endless hallways
I am a stranger myself,
ignorant and scared.
I only know that your monkeys
are descending, tearing apart
your vital stuffing, and flinging
it over unknown fields.
You have set yourself on fire,
and each piece of your sand
peers out of a clogged hourglass,
building up slowly inside
until the upper half threatens to break.
Let it flow freely again,
in your time, on your watch,
beyond this dark castle.

Tracks

Eyes near and far,
in my college classroom,
track her, zero in on her tattoos:
cat prints evenly spaced,
deliberate as black ink,
more vivid than the text she is bent over.
Paw impressions climb up her bare back,
scramble over her shoulder and vanish under straps.
Another line of claw-pads runs up her arm,
originating on her hand, where the designs
crouch in a cluster, then set out
on an indelible journey over skin.

All beasts converge; where an imaginary animal
left permanent marks a real one might do the same
someday, eyes hot on her trail.
Speaking loudly, I call attention to my scrawls
on the white board.

Masks

Self-exiled to the back,
desk by desk he moved
another row each day,
nearer to the front,
to the words read aloud,
to their fronts and sides and backs.

Up close, his shoulder length black hair
kept him underground, his mask
combed straight down,
eclipsing dark Native eyes, Native skin.

"I am ugly," he whispered to me,
his breath ruffling the curtain of hair,
parted only for *The Phantom of the Opera*
and "The Minister's Black Veil."

Smoke and Fire

Smoke penetrated each piece,
inflaming the music teacher:
reed ruined, mouthpiece choked,
valves clogged, gagged.

Weekly he cleaned the instrument,
warned her—who sat in back,
said nothing—not to smoke cigarettes.
She wouldn't quit.

Incensed,
driving down roads that were barely roads,
after much searching at night,
he found her parents' home:
a desert campfire circled
by charred rocks, plastic milk crates,
sun-bleached tents fraying
at the stakes, flaps bedraggled.

He stood silent in the shadows, listening.
Before a crackling chorus of flames,
she practiced,
her saxophone on fire.

Grass Dancer in the Desert

For Don Cachora
Quechan Reservation

Geronimo's descendent will get to my class on time.
From the open doorway
I watch him navigating on foot
a labyrinth of water, a controlled flooding,
the weekly irrigation of our school's flat grounds.

He shuns narrow, elevated sidewalks,
bounds over stagnant pools.

Graceful and adroit,
a grass dancer at heart,
he lands where the grass endures,
leaping from island
to shrinking island,
no easy feat
upon receding tribal land.

Facing Them

In the foreground of a Southwest painting
human figures form a broken line
across parallel lines of green
running clear and neat to the horizon.
Field workers without faces face the viewer.
They're covered by red and blue bandanas,
by company caps pulled down
over shaded eyes, the bright logos up,
well-rendered. Masked, bound in work clothes
in the wide-open field, they resemble
banditos robbed daily, hourly,
by the endless rows of cash crops.

In the background, a vivid sky;
up close, specks of brown paint show skin
through holes in flannel and denim.
One figure tries to stand tall
in clumsy, oversized rubber boots,
stares out of the tight framework
at the art goers. Two turn sideways,
bend down, eye dirt and something beyond
dirt. The last one lifts to the light
bagged lettuce already chopped.

At the Top

A man at the top of a palm tree
cuts away his cover.
The height to which he has climbed,
spiking upwards,
loses its foliage.

Frond after frond
plummets
into a green pile below,
dust rising suddenly
in swirling migrations.

All afternoon he works,
hacks at gigantic fans,
revealing himself piecemeal:
boots, pants, bandana, straw hat.

Now he stands exposed,
belted in place,
facing bark,
yet leaning precariously out—

in the direction of the country
he left years ago.

Three Views of an Alley
Yuma, Arizona

1.
I keep an eye on the economy,
evident everyday
in the alley behind my house.

There, slow cars pull up,
and stuff fit for an alley
finds a home inside,

across the laps of children
packed into the back seat:
boards, tires, boxes, paint buckets.

2.
Through red wood slats,
through the spaces my fence affords,
I see pieces of the needy,

fragments of the poor, foraging,
the pieces never cohering fully
until all the parts are out of sight, if then.

3.
A narrow dirt road,
the alley runs for blocks and blocks,
oblivious to intersecting main streets,

through the city's heart,
offering—if I step into it—
a diminishing perspective of dumpsters,

a view of successive shrinking bins,
mostly empty black vessels
to which people,

heads bent, shuffle,
hoping for anything to eat or sell.

Desert Drama

In my idling box seat,
I, a captive audience of one,
watch a guard rail rise,
lights snap off,
and a freight train lurch away
like an iron curtain.

Desperate actors,
revealed on the other side,
stand stunned, fraught
with fear and relief, waterless.
The troupe disbands
as border agents approach.

Solo now, each scatters
off a cindery stage
in different directions,
in search of water, food, rest,
words, new roles.

The Living and the Dead:
Halloween/ Dia de Los Muertos

Knock, ring. Knock, ring.

Curls like black halos,
round faces painted bone white,
maidenly dresses the color of fresh blood,
bright pink bags, enormous
and empty, gaping below me:
two sweet little girls,
two dead little girls,
twins doubled, all four of them
wide-eyed and staring.

We share a silence.
Crossing the threshold,
I offer them all the candy.

Edge of Air and Space

Drama Hunger

International Wolf Center,
Ely, Minnesota

The captive audience in place,
suspense builds.

Timber wolves wait in the wings,
in holding cages where they stand
and stretch,
sniffing the meaty air.

The stage manager swings a plastic bucket
near their noses,
then scatters red scraps
across a fenced-in forest,
tucks morsels under logs,
slings offal into wild, wild weeds.

Finally released, the Dramatis Personae
scramble down stage right,
up stage left, dead center.

Behind thick glass, our eyes devour them,
the sumptuous fur, the fat tongues.
We love to sit back
and lick our chops.

Gray heads down, the wolves nose the chow
and gulp it; there is nothing else,
no denouement, no dessert,
leaving us famished for more.

Cataclysm

The birdbath reposed in the shadow of passing
colors like classical sculpture. Circled by peonies,
roses, morning glories, chrysanthemums,
it centered my neighbor's garden,
its pedestal shaped like a Greek column,
the marble basin an open spa for birds.

Leaves, petals, snow, rain, hail,
each in its turn, gathered here.
Cloud images floated across the surface,
an elm mirrored in miniature, a star buoyant.

Once, shouldering this world,
my friends and I heaved it over,
snapped its neck, spilt
sky, seasons, our reflections,
and cracked the solid offering of water.

Burrowed

All that high labor was lost on me,
the gathering, the carrying,
by teeth and claws, of leaves and twigs,
the building and securing.

I didn't know a squirrel nest existed
until the elm lost half itself in a storm,
all its leaves fallen, revealing
a roughhewn basket, a home on a limb
surrounded by tree top spaces.
I am too taken up with the ground.

Hunger and Need

Dugs dragging over grass,
a grey cat with a closed eye,
collarless, stares at me
with the open one
as I pig out on pizza.

Toppings are suddenly tasteless,
cheese turning cold,
cardboard box an oily grey shadow,
too many red pepper flakes on my tongue.

I spit them out, close the lid, open it—
both eyes are on me.

Naturalist

My cat brings out the savior in me.
From his claws I pulled a quivering red flame,
a cardinal whose tail feathers broke loose
in my hand. From his teeth
I ripped a half-flayed baby rabbit free,

liberated a goldfinch that hobbled off on one wing.
I relocated a garter snake, punctured, far from
his subterranean nest, shook a half-gulped salamander out,
tailless.

Now my cat shuns my hand, sleeps at the end
of the bed, or in another room, won't eat dry food.
He too, naturally, despises me.

Tarantulas

Here on the heart of my hand
is a black entanglement,
a fugitive from a freak show,
an optical illusion of legs/fingers
stepping/groping as one
in all directions at once.

I plucked him
from the desert east of Yuma.
He can be anything now:
a furry shadow eclipsing my lifeline,
perhaps a war-hobbled, crutch-laden soldier,
or a pianist's arching fingers
playing my nerves like ancient notes.

In my hand
another one trembles,
reaching toward the edge of air and space,
searching for its lost body.

Getting to the Heart

He was above me.
But like knowledge or love,
all I knew were bits,
bark-like pieces,
dark fragments pinging in a gutter,
raining down on me
from the gabled roof.

Soon my sundeck was
littered with puzzle shards
like chips of memory,
scattered remnants of experience—
I find them everywhere.

When I looked up,
a squirrel, walnut in mouth,
was gnawing
the heart of the matter.

The Flight of Flowers

As we waited for a bus in Mexico,
we beheld Birds of Paradise,

clustered and riding high,
all reds and blues,
in the back of a pick-up truck,

the sublime cargo shifting
from end to battered end,
a wild garden wavering,

spirited through traffic,
a special delivery.

Word Flood Down Below

Midway down the dark stairs,
Tolstoy, Conrad,
James, Goethe, and Wolfe drifted—

words on water,
luminous prose on blackness,
their depths sinking slowly
into my flooded basement floor.

Into this library I waded,
books receding, ebbing away,
as I splashed and slogged toward geniuses.

Condemned to stand in a pool,
Tantalus reached forever
for fruit he couldn't pick.

But I grabbed dissolving verse,
satires separating from their spines,
their covers like sodden wings,
sputtering novellas, resigned elegies.

I breathed on words, into words,
to dry them, revive them.
I stacked Shakespeare on high pipes,
stuffed paperbacks in my pockets,
dragged anthologies ashore.
Dozens capsized.
In his garden Monet
painted water lilies on a shimmering surface.
I dredge the rising underworld for the drowned.

Home Decor

Pursuit of a bargain brought us to this bone yard:
Lake Superior driftwood bleached and petrified,
and scattered along the shore like ruins,
or roughly formed into arrested waves on rocks.

Stumbling over them, we scrounge for the perfect
piece, twisted, strange and angular,
and stripped of green origins, of leaf and root.
We want the abstract design, the pure shape
on our mantel or coffee table, bone-like and sterile.

Artifice

The wolf artwork standing in the lobby,
between potted ferns,
draws me to glass.
Before such creations,
I always check for holes,
tell-tale points of entry—
arrows, steel teeth, bullets
in the stuffed wild.

But I can't see any flaws, can't detect
where death entered and exited,
the luxurious black, grey and white fur
neatly brushed, wavy
like a simulated winter storm,
the ends teased up to suggest
a cold wind in a vacuum or a shrill cry.

The art of the afterlife is so tidy,
So perfect, I want to howl.

A Speechless Skyful

Yuma, Arizona

A dawn of discharges:
the season opens with a solitary pop,
then a chorus of them,
muffled volleys flying from afar.

All morning I hear distant shots—
in fields of stubble toy guns sounding off.

All day and night
doves, winged symbols,
fall from a speechless sky.

Dangerous Beauty

No end to it: a birch tree bound in bittersweet,
the climbing kind, an aspiring parasite,
orange-red berries snaking
around white bark, a beautiful
strangulation from trunk to crown.

I pulled: one unraveling led to other ravelings,
all one convoluted strand, a self-made
Gordian knot tightening above my knife,
beyond my vine-gathering
and wreath-making skills.
Some bittersweet is out of reach.

Ghost

A thin branch reaching toward my window,
even a trembling leaf,
sets off sensor lights.
A cat cutting diagonally
across the driveway
brings down shafts of gold-white.
A floating candy wrapper
illuminates half the yard.
A strong wind trips the light fantastic.

Sensitive things
with minds of their own,
they detect everything except me.
I stride below spotlights,
retrace my steps, yet the bulbs
don't notice, remain dark.
I am invisible, without substance,
insignificant in their scheme,
as if I installed the stars myself,
and they know me well enough.

Final Solution

I followed the directions like a Boy Scout.
The application of death was clear:
two tablespoons full,
but do not disturb the ant hill.

Never have I been so gentle.
Crouched over the colony,
I tilted the spoon,
jiggled poison,

and dry specks rained down,
yellowing the air.
Some of the bits tumbled toward the center
and entered the hole,
clogging the opening in the ground.

I have never been so delicate.
Most granules decorated the outer rim
like candy sprinkles on a sand cake.
Another tilt of the spoon
conjured up hundreds to the party,
to the confetti.

Prudent I was.
Spoon poised over the teeming mound,
I kept my distance—
no toxicity on my skin.

I did not disturb the formation,
worked smooth and banked high,
and fanned out in a half-circle
like a miniature amphitheater
meticulously silenced.

Eye of the Hurricane

We put our hope in candles,
in the utility ones—
stout columns casting a practical glow.

But they were gone, seized at the store,
bought by a nervous storm of shoppers.
All that was left for us were religious candles,

row on row on the otherwise empty shelves,
each glass container decorated
with images of Our Lady of Guadalupe,

herself a light surrounded
by painted auras and painted flames,
a tiny wick atop a foot of wax.

We bought it.
Her likeness topped our television
flickering with changing weather reports,

and we waited for the darkness,
braced for blackout,
our eyes turning again and again
to a small flame.

Feeder

Somehow this hummingbird feeder
stood its ground in midair,
in 80 mile per hour winds that downed power
lines, blackened homes and sheared off roofs.
Somehow it maintained a foothold, a handhold.

Bright yellow, with red flowers painted on glass,
its Buddha-like belly awash in juice,
the feeder swung wildly on a string and survived—
a carnival trinket dangling above
ancient mesquite and ironwood trees
toppled like twigs.

We found it attached to a patio beam,
amidst broken limbs and scattered cement blocks.
Above the rubble a red sweetness endured,
held out like an offering to the suddenly bereaved.

Its bright inner life, in the gloom,
was still visible, alluring.
We—displaced from our home,
adrift on the streets—hovered near,
supped on the red sight, drew it in heartily.

Uncountable

You stand on a rock, pointing.
When they clear the trees
and soar into view,
you start counting,
zero in on the first twelve,
the next six, numbering
Canadian geese quickly
in your head.
Your lips barely move.

But soon you forget the tally,
despite tying knots
in your mind
or fingering beads,
all to help you remember
where you left off
in the flow.
You lose your place.

They are now
miles upriver,
lettering the sky loosely,
ribboning in and out
of each other.

Light Seeds

Ignored,
mowed, poisoned,
when did dandelions go?
Now their seedlings
blossom in air.

Occupying our vision,
they float freely, *en masse*, drifting
like May snow across our streets,
then spiriting over houses and trees—
torn white veils, feather down
from an immense passing bird.

On their way a few seed clouds cling,
if only for moments,
to my dark window screens
like the stuff of light.

The Uses of the Dead

Tracked on, the bear
carpeted our cabin,
spread-eagled on the floor
as if fallen from a great height
and anchored,
a coffee table centered on his back.

Chairs were arranged
around his frayed edges,
where adults talked
about fishing and hunting
over his skull, glass eyes fixed
on a blackened hearth.

I played with the bear,
my fingers stepping gingerly
into a gaping mouth:
an intrepid explorer shadowed
by rows of stalagmites and stalactites.

At night he was my bed,
a sleeping bag unfurled
as if in the heart of a wild black forest.

There, knowing the uses of the dead,
I could fly, riding his skin.

Black Flowering

For my friends' amusement,
and from a sharp impulse,
the knife I threw impaled to bark
a large bat asleep on a green bough.

A crucified awakening,
two screams,
and then a sudden, black flowering of wings.
My bloodshot eyes blinking wildly,
quivering in a cold, dark place,
I hung upside down inside.

Against the Current
Winona, Minnesota

At the far end
of Latch Island,
we saw leaves on water,
a bushy crown,
an emerald-haired river god
emerging, rising slowly.

The full headdress was buoyant,
yet fixed. Still connected
to its splintered trunk on shore,
the fallen tree rode the Mississippi in place.

We swam upriver for it,
this floating, anchored nest,
changing styles constantly
(butterfly, breaststroke, back stroke)
muscling the current that bullied us
backwards, sideways, down.

We wanted our tree to hold and keep us,
to entwine limbs in branches,
our hands in leaves,
to fight for our watery position.

But when we thrashed into the nest,
grabbed the crown, dragonflies flew up—
a cloud with a thousand wings,
a dark firestorm
pelting and blinding us.

We let go.

Strange Afterlife

Candy in hand, I rounded the store's corner,
counting the blessings in my bag,
when a chicken escaped
from the back of the old market.

Stark white, sans head, the hen
zigzagged across gravel
toward breakneck traffic.
I froze—all eyes, all disbelief.

As if his life depended on recovery,
on recapture, the butcher gave chase,
in pursuit of wings, drumsticks, breasts.

But the fowl errant
ran away with what was left,
outdistancing him,
then circled back, halfway, spewing blood.

In a red -stained white frock,
a hand strained toward a headless creation,
desperate for the body
as I would be someday for the bread and wine.

Flaws

Outsiders
with inside lives,
leathery green lizards,
small as roaches,
thrive in the cracks of our patio deck,
in the imperfections of garage and house.
Gaps, rents, breaks, rifts,
these reptilia claim as home become
vantage points from which to view
our interiors and exteriors.
Sudden as insights, silent as witnesses,
they flourish in our flaws,
in constructions neither true nor plumb.

Minimum Wage

Slugs eat holes in our collard greens,
so many tears the once-hardy leaves
are half air.

Golden beetles steal from strawberries,
siphon juice,
or whiten raspberries,
red bled as if from hearts.

Mature grape leaves turn, in a devouring time,
to overworked lace, brittle and brown;
nothing to offer, pick, and savor.

What's next? Belabored carrots?
Exploited Bok Choy? Stressed beans?

Our garden is a feast for parasites,
an insect capitalism at work—
we eat leftovers.

Where to Find Wildlife in Minnesota

Off Highway 61,
check out the trash barrels
along the Mississippi River.
Raccoons will stare up at you.
Tip the bin over for a closer view.

Pull into a Duluth gas station
and park next to a black bear,
spread-eagled on the hood of a Jeep.
You can touch it while filling up.

Walk the old wagon wheel bridge
outside of Winona
and see eel and gar writhing on the defunct road.
Leave them there! Garbage fish.

At the bottom of dumpsters in Rochester,
elegant deer legs,
sawed off,
grow longer or shorter,
depending, every time you look.

For fascinating remnants—dark green,
intricately patterned, pottery-like—
exam my neighbor's driveway.
He loves to park the wheels of his sports car
on the massive shells of migrating turtles.

Scour the mowed ditches for pheasants,
shredded like Oriental fans,
or stare up at the heads
staring down at you in any bar.

Look in a mirror,
look at pictures of yourself as a teenager.
Don't bother with the North Woods.
You won't see wildlife there.

Ghosting the Pages

Transfiguration

The cold took it away,
my marriage ring,
a loose fit from the start,
loosening even more
as I swam through frigid water
(my flesh shriveling to the bone)
and made widening water rings.

Unnoticed, it slipped off,
discovered missing
when I struck sand.
Somewhere at the bottom
diamonds are sparkling upward
in the muck, a sea change for two.

Opening and Closing

At Miller's bar in St. Paul, now closed

It sounded like a door opening and closing
against an object,
muffled somewhat in the women's restroom,
where Jimmy the bartender had followed
his wife as if he used both
whenever he felt a need.

The howling juke box,
cranked up even more,
chased away the screams.
We leaned back into the oblivion
of a pounding song.

Frozen on stools,
we cursed our clenched jaws,
brooded,
stared into open, mirrored rooms.

She exited first,
her face opened and closed.
Then out strode Jimmy,
going straight
to work behind the bar,
tidying up,
scrubbing mugs
and twisting a bar rag
(two red fingers tamping it down)
into the socket of a shot glass.

Shards

For some reason we marveled as we argued
about how far broken glass flies
and what it resembles: a framed spider web,
a crumbling mosaic, a two-room floor puzzle,
twin stars ground underfoot.
We were poets.

No pieces are big and chunky,
overlapped like stacked ice floes,
nothing so easy to clean up.
Tempered window glass holds its designs,
falling bit by bit over time.
We don't forget.

Sweeping together again,
we find fragments everywhere,
hidden in cracks, along base boards,
in plants, clothes, hair.
Some breakage, we agree,
will remain unseen.

Dress Rehearsal

Whenever my parents fought, often and loud,
I never knew why, only that
my father dressed up in a herringbone
tweed suit, donned a tie, a brown felt
hat with a black band,
sported cufflinks, a blue vest, a pocket watch.

Once properly attired, he pulled from deep within
their bedroom closet a suitcase already packed,
and trudged with it downstairs,
standing fixed by the front door he never opened,
standing in the rain of his tears,
a damp, elegant stranger as if newly arrived,
perhaps a gentleman visitor,
or a travelling salesman lugging heavy wares—
my mother suddenly enamored.

Life Savings

On the suicide of a fellow cabbie

On a nightstand
beside his made bed,
they found his payroll checks,
neatly stacked
under a burned-out light,
a half year's worth
chronologically ordered
from June to December
from a now defunct cab company—
still sealed in blue envelopes,
unopened, undisturbed.

Housing Project Labor Force

In my neighbor's backyard, bicycle parts
heaped and scattered: chains, fenders,
banana seats, handlebars, sprockets.
It's a family enterprise, with daily
pickups and drop-offs
stretching from streets to parks to homes—
a conveyor belt, assembly line and
division of labor in one.

Such an industrious lot, and there is a pounding
in their basement, iron on metal, as if Norse dwarfs
were working overtime all the time,
but not for Sigurd.
No magical swords. Stolen dreams dismantled,
reconstructed piece by piece, spray painted
and sold at cut rate prices so black-market buyers
can ride them for a while—no handed.

Dubbed

The film seems like a foursome.
Two couple romantically,
while unseen others,
another pair,
speak for the visible
(and maybe each other)
in distant voices, in different tongues.

Even the audience is involved.
They know that between
those bodies and the disembodied,
between acts without words
and words without acts,
we truly love doubly, disjointedly—
here and elsewhere,
on-screen and off.

Ghosting the Pages

History in my hand:
a small blue address book decades old,
phone numbers included,
found in a forgotten drawer in my desk.

Here's a number
I could not live without
until it became unlisted,
and here's one
I circled with red ink
again and again.
It isn't working now.

Here's a former friend,
his number's crossed out
for reasons crossed out in my head.
Another pal changed his name
and now he's off the record.

Always moving then,
an old lover has a series
of addresses, a timeline, a map,
leading to blank pages
at the end of my book.

I turn back.
Like a jealous lover,
I trace the imprint of a number,
ink faded,
the impressions rising slowly,
ghosting the page.

The Colors of Ex Nihilo

For C. Gilbertson

In his basement workshop
he constructs stained glass windows
and still talks about a time:
home from grade school,
he opened the front door to no one home.
Nothing confronted him.

He walked from room to room,
emptiness to emptiness,
felt its weight, a heaviness.

The house never seemed so spacious,
full of his footsteps
echoing,
full of his voice
echoing.

Closets gaped at him—toys gone.
Light bulbs removed.
Paper plates, plastic forks and spoons
cleared from cupboards.

He saw scratches on the wood floor,
permanent marks
where furniture once stood,
worn couches with deep depressions,
springs broken.

Finally risen
from the sagging cushions,
his parents in a day packed up
and moved without telling him,
forgetting....

Vacancy still faces him in his basement,

so he cuts glass, puzzles pieces
together into soldered designs,
trying to shape glazed color,
blues mostly, and light.

Heirloom

The Singer Sewing Machine
never sang in our house,
transformed upon arrival
into a vanity topped with glass,
mirror- backed, and covered
with ruffled chintz—
a Victorian dress.

An elaborate wrap,
belled out to the floor,
silenced bobbins, shuttles, fly wheel,
all the hard inner parts.

The heirloom still worked
and mother could sew,
but I never heard a staccato needle
or saw a crinkled Butterick pattern.

Grandmother treadled here.
Mother retired the Singer,
applied make-up,
brushed her hair.
Maybe she hid the machine
because it was her mother's,
and she didn't want to remember
needles, scraps, patterns.

Once I lifted the dress
and touched iron.

Walks of Life

For Warren, each step forward
initiated another one sideways.
His left foot walked straight ahead,
while his right veered to the right,

suddenly, like a bird falling out of formation,
a band member limping out of a parade,
or a small animal hobbling off a road.

In the hallways four students,
inspired, aped his polio.

Their crooked line twisted behind him
to geometry, civics, P.E., lunch:
left/right, forward/sideways, straight/slant,
a synchronized dance accompanied
by a laughing audience,
a running act much of the school year.

Eventually, wearing down, he found
solace with his cane, swung it,
thrust it like a wooden sword
at the merry troupe of hoofers.

But nothing deterred them.
When he was absent, after
he was gone, they followed in his footsteps
every step of their lives.

Freewheeling

My young neighbor knows what day denies
night permits. So he waits until the moon is high,

when the pavements he relies on
call him out, and then goes freewheeling

in his wheelchair over empty streets,
empty sidewalks, across forbidden church cement,

in and out of reserved office parking
spaces, down private drives, his head up,

his arms outstretched—flying
in a permanent place, and from it.

Recycling an Open Dump—1956

In memory of my grandmother

Rust inspired her—
a sunset on an ice box,
fiery tin cans,
iron bed springs turning rose.

She augmented red with crimson,
baby blue with aqua blue,
her eyes drawn to shapes:
chipped teacups, amber apothecary bottles,
a broken rocker.

Stroke by stroke, she salvaged a washboard,
reclaimed a bread box, a crippled bicycle, a rag doll.

Her easel on the edge of a sunken world,
the abandoned found a home on her canvasses,
housed eventually within elegant frames.

Love in the Western World

Riding a rocker,
my aunt travels with saddlebags full of stories,
and says my uncle dragging his silver spurs
across a bunkhouse floor
sparked her interest.

And says my grandparents
courted on horseback,
and flushed from riding,
galloped home late at night.

She says grandpa
herded a dozen cattle
across a rearing Montana river.
He and horse swept away
righted themselves,
and then he tied rope to saddle horn
to longhorns and pulled each one out.

No work backtracker,
he hung chaps, bandana, Stetson hat,
vest, shirt, jeans, and gun
on barbed wire to dry.

And in the wild running prairie grass,
Grandpa, wearing only cowboy boots,
not waiting on the sun to do its job,
fixed a fence broken
for as far as the naked eye could see.
My aunt rocks West again and again.
I trot behind.

Atlas

For Barbara

On your lap now is Minnesota—
North Woods, lakes, rivers,
Blooming Prairie, Belle Plain, Iron Range.

A glance is all I need to know my place,
and I cannot stop glancing.
Maps are irresistible.

Slowly you turn back the country,
and Iowa appears, spread out,
and then Colorado, California, Alabama.
It could be any state— when I look at you,
I am never lost.

The Student Who Launched Pencils
Inspired by Tom Stoa

He sized up a crowded classroom,
scanned cloudy blackboards,
read the atmosphere.

Then, meticulous, aligned his pencil
half on, half off
the edge of a marked desk,
brought the tip of his concentration
to bear on yellow wood,
and with two fingers striking down
sent it soaring.

I watched in desk-bound awe.
Climbing, the pencil cleared
ordered heads front
to back, back to front,
and dim fluorescent lights
hung from a sound-proof ceiling.

Eyes followed its flight.
Our teacher, back turned, droned on,
oblivious to the slim acrobat,
the aerodynamics of lead,
a skywriter, a fragment of color
completing a rainbow arc.

I squirmed in an assigned seat.
The pencil landed safely, intact,
five rows over,
in an aisle of its own—

someday, in lieu of pencils,
the student would launch words.

Breaking Up

At the top I lose an angel, then a shepherd.
Candy canes, horns and bells
plummet next, and a twisted string of lights
falls with crystal ornaments,
gifts to each other. Finally,
I fumble a star.

Half the celestial order
as we knew it on earth
lands in your lap,
where you pack
on the floor,
in old newspapers,
what we have put up together
for seven Christmases.

We are down to a tree,
dark as an eclipse.
The stubborn trunk clings to a flimsy stand.
How do we remove this dry skeleton
without littering our lives
or scratching our faces?

Funeral Relatives

In memory of K.H.

They show up first, at last,
to see what is left:
you in a box.

Yes, they are here,
though they have missed
the other services in your life,
the ones you celebrated
alone, the ones you shared with others:

haunted Vietnam soldier
turned anti-war protester,
high school dropout
turned college graduate,
teacher, husband, father.

Now you are in a pinstripe suit
you hated, a black tie
instead of a red bandana
wrapped around wild, curly hair;
hands overlapped
instead of clenched.

This is nothing new.
They have stuffed you
into other compartments
that tightened
over the years,

taking them down
at times to confirm
what they already knew about you,
or perhaps to push the contents
into a dark corner.

You were not a good fit
for their constructions,
so you had to be rearranged
(a shake here, a slam there)

so you would fit,
and fit you did, in their minds.

They love containers,
but the one before them now
weighs on their spirits.
It is too obvious,
too prominent, for their style.

What they feel about you now
they have already felt,
and so they stuffed themselves
into themselves long ago.

Yes, they are here at last.
The trouble is, you are not,
learning early in life
how to escape from boxes.

Eight-Balled

"Toss the pool ball. I'll catch it,"
coaxed my friend.
I did.

But—ball in air—
he stepped aside,
exited the Y,
his smile lingering
in the space he left—
a ghostly cat's grin.

My lob initiated a black trajectory,
a perfect, dark arc,
the white-circled 8

revolving slowly, enormously,
still legible from
the gaming room,
a rogue planet spinning out of orbit,

out of bounds.
The sphere struck red foyer tiles,
ricocheted into a second arc,
and gaining newfound momentum,
shattered glass over a white-haired secretary

writing behind an office window,
her paperwork suddenly dangerous,
her expression breaking up,
like a friendship over which
a disembodied grin still hangs.

Tracking
For Barbara

Buying online, a high-tech hunter of gemstones,
I track a moss agate
(smoky amber swirls inside a smooth luminosity)
from Milan to New York
to Northfield to a bronze necklace
around your opal neck.
Shipped, delivered, this rock is from the heart.

Sculptor

One of those pocketknife men,
gone now like their dress hats,
my father carried his knife everywhere,
in dark trousers matching suits and vests.

In his collegiate attire he knew it well:
grooved sheath, bark-like;
single blade's spine,
baby finger length and crescent shape.
It never touched keys or coins.

A gentleman, he put the knife
to himself, picking teeth,
scraping under nails,
extracting wax,
as if sculpting himself.

He squeezed the knife like a charm,
worried it smooth like a stone,
pointed it toward a childhood
carved out of poverty,
whittling away the memory
of who he is
and where he came from.

Two Doors

Two doors I opened simultaneously,
one to a boarding house hallway,
carpet flowers worn thin.

In the narrow corridor without pictures,
I heard my neighbor spit tobacco juice
into a bedside coffee can,
a ringing hollowness brimming
with darkness in time.

A woman on the other side
screamed through a taut chain-lock opening
at my passing form,
her unlit Christmas tree up year round
in a corner.

Another tenant,
an insomniac with a skin disease,
trod the flowers end to end,
once entering my room at night
(a shadow sensed in sleep)
to tell me I had forgotten to lock the door.

Tacked high on the inside
of the door, a Mary Oliver poem opened—
and opened me— into a world of struggle
and suffering, the speaker striving for
passage through a swamp,
 a "dry stick" sprouting, branching out,
transforming her life,
step by mucky step,
into "a breathing palace of leaves"
rooted in a bog.

We lived together for two years.
I read it every time I went out,
every time I came in—
and it read me.

Weight of a Lost World

Break Time

Break time in the Cry House:
a Bird Singer's turquoise gourd rattle,
just shaken in song, in grief,
recovers on a pew.

Scattered farther down, other colored rattles,
filled with dried seeds,
wait to be lifted.

All their long, worn, wooden handles
yearn to be raised in rhythm.

Ears need to be filled.
Empty water bottle in hand,
I wait for choral chants—

my student Cecilia silent in a coffin,
whose smile was a dance,
whose laugh was a song.

Keeping My Balance

My kid bike passed its prime at six years—
handlebar grips gone,
sprocket missing teeth,
blue paint scratched off
as if by the fingernails of time.

Yet I rode it,
attached to the old bike like decorative decals
on dented fenders. Repaired tires:
a red patchwork of mishaps and adventures.

I adjusted in flight. When the chain lurched,
slipped, I rode out a falling sensation,
sudden nothing, arrested movement,
interrupted cycle.

Driven, I balanced in hiatus,
like last night when I took an extra step up
on a dark, aging staircase,
or when I walked into clear patio glass
to open blue sky.

Spatial Rearrangements

At first sight,
she sinks with the sunken,
her childhood farm home caved in,
interring itself slowly
during her forty-year absence.

She takes stock
of what time has taken,
walks from field to grass
to flattened roof.
She knows the unoccupied
collapses, the unused goes
to waste, feels like a ghost
returning to ghosts,
a survivor to a ruined survivor.

Her vision is turned upside down:
a bedroom window,
once offering a meadow view,
leans in a root cellar.
A broken vanity mirror
reflects a piece of sky and a dirt floor.
Rain has scarred overdue
library books
and movie magazines,
the stars darkened, fallen—
Hedy Lamar, Veronica Lake, Rita Hayworth—
their once porcelain cheeks
shriveled on moldy pages.

She salvages what she can,
a three-pane window,
paints the wood,
later presses wildflowers
between extra panes.

Now a triptych of a meadow
in late bloom hangs high
on her living room wall.

Grafting

I was a home.
Now I'm a house:
120 years old,
1100 square feet,
three bedrooms,
a garage, a porch.
I've been listed.

My family, their clutter gone,
abandon me in a moment's notice,
let outsiders in.

Never been so clean,
and for strangers—
open house visitations all day.
My floors groan, hinges creak.

Buyers wolf cookies,
ogle flowers everywhere—
a funeral parlor.

Added wall mirrors
artfully hung enhance space,
project depth where
there is little room.
Nothing sells like an illusion.

It's theater.
Walk-ons walk in and out,
scripts in mind,
plans for my improvement,
modernization,
a gutting of a vintage kitchen
in the works.

Still, I stand my ground—

original fixtures preserved,
unpainted wood,
oak floors aslant,
a stamped tin ceiling
with a few water stains.
Character means real cracks.

Banded

From curiosity which is never simple
(inquiry gives rise to indiscretion,
to bedside inquisition) I ask
about the medical bracelets on your arms,
two sets of carnival-like rings,
two split rainbows of specific warnings.

By request, you read your wraparound
fate that slides neither up or down,
fastened always in place: Fall Risk,
Limb Alert, Allergy, Restricted
Extremity, and a purple band you don't read,
with the capital letters DNR.

Later, on the way down, I see
the words Do Not Resuscitate
in a sealed room, in a dark shaft,
and descend, breathless.

Specifics

In memoriam—Wes Streeter (1950-2018)

Death brings you to life—now I remember
everything I forgot about you.

An electric train you engineered off the tracks,
crashed into a plastic tunnel, flew off a painted mountain.
Wrestling matches in the living room,
lamps falling, your father pulling his belt out
slowly like a long black snake.

Singing punks, we impersonated the Jets and
Sharks from *West Side Story*
"... and we're gonna beat
Every last buggin' gang on the whole buggin' street"
snapped fingers, flashed invisible switchblades,
the neighbors amused, our parents aghast.

Your angry big brother throwing our bikes skyward,
wheels cycling up, down. Rocking
a workbench, riding it standing like a bronco,
breaking my toe. Red tears, the only ones
I witnessed, wrung from your eyes when your sister,
cutting a boat rope upwards, fatally plunged
a knife into her throat.

The details dog me. Reading *War and Peace* in bed,
in your pajamas, in the afternoon—a cigarette
burning in your mouth, ashes on white sheets,
on page after page. Dostoevsky's *The Possessed*
possessed you. My manuscript you tried to steal,
publish in your name, the story finally rejected
in my name—- pissed yet flattered, I didn't
know whether to hit or hug you.

Relentless, the particulars, this memorial:

Dartmouth drop out,
a Vietnam-era conscience nixing an
ROTC scholarship.
The weed you gave me, The Doors
and Hendrix rocking our heads senseless.
Petitioning—no, hounding—a Catholic college
to serve beer in the student union, and proud,
elated that the throaty taps spurted and gushed.

Much later, your music promotions appeared
somewhere—Iris DeMent, Ralph Stanley,
The Flying Burrito Brothers—
and your name at the bottom of a wind-battered
Film Society advertisement—*Apocalypse Now*—
in a dark cellar window, and rough years
of vague drifting apart.

The specifics stick like darts.
Your afterlife haunts precisely.
I am talking to myself, to you, to the dead.

Lost and Found
Stillwater, Minnesota

The knock on our door—a summons served,
a call to action when no course of action was clear.
Pictures were presented, mostly black and white,
but who can find the forever lost?

Dementia hustled her outside,
from nursing home to winter night.
Each step lost in the act of stepping.
Nothing in front, nothing behind.
A step at a time all the time.

Whirling snow deranged her tracks,
yet our lights turned out for her—
flashlights, car lights, flares, lanterns.
Every house lamp set on high.

We were all light lost in the lights of others,
beacons scanning ourselves,
fireflies swarming each other,
blinded in the black hole of her absence.

Out of alignment all night,
the stars in our brains sizzled out.
 Only the thawing spring would reveal her.
"April is the cruelest month."
But she followed a memory of light.
Seated in a bar, she sipped golden beer,
slowly, in no hurry to be found.

Raft

In memory of Cecilia

Why did you do it?
Why did you jump raft?

You knew well its roughhewn craftsmanship,
everything tied together
with hurried knots that held fast, that persevered.
Humor and conscience, you said,
propelled the timbers.

You knew well its humanity,
Huck and Jim on a floating stage,
creating dialogue,
crossing boundaries together toward unmapped regions of
becoming.

I saw those characters emerge vividly
from your writing's crossties.
I heard them clearly
in your essay's buoyant words.

Why did you abandon Huck and Jim,
who were your true kin?
You dove into darkness
and swam toward the coldest shore.

Sky and Earth Report

For E. L. February 10ᵗʰ, 2017

1.
Tonight, at 7:55 a Snow Moon will rise,
a Hunger Moon to Native Americans,
signifying winter hardships,
followed by a penumbra lunar eclipse
at 8:50, and in the early hours
a green New Year Comet will appear,
travelling for five years to be seen, beheld.

We will drive to the dark places to see the lights.

2.
Today, at 1:00 p.m. you were raised
by a Hoyer so you could use the bathroom,
then, returned to bed, lifted again
via another machine, and eased into a wheelchair,
pushed up a ramp into an ambulance
and driven to the next intensive care unit
thirty miles away, arriving at 2:30.

We saw you depart, two riding with you, all the lights on.

3.
Tonight, we will be true stargazers,
will train naked eyes,
refract vision into two realms,
split sight between sky and earth.

Driven

Like others, I hate it,
driving at night,
the once starry blacktop
that guided me,
leading me on and on,
topped with darkness now,
a tar of night.

When did that other country road fade?
Dim headlights on high,
I see via sign and symbol,
ghost lines, a form crossing
before me, its red eyes reflecting my own.

I can't go back, don't want to go forward.
Out there, night fields flourish.
Here, everyone wants to go home,
driven more than driving,
the wheel turning our hands.

The Figure on the Wall

Some of them are recognizable, even known
by their touch, cold, blunt, metallic:
the instruments you sit with as you wait
in a small room for the specialist,
as unknown as the tools at his disposal.
The instruments know themselves, their purposes,
and your body better than you do
at this time, which feels like the last time.

A ghostly x-ray reveals the fractured bones
of a spirit, presumably yours but you aren't sure
what is yours or others', and what is
internal, otherworldly, or illusory.
Is this hell or limbo? Consider the human figure on the
wall, for instance, a standing body
pictured in outline, who somehow
manages to hold illustrated organs inside,
though they are exposed to whoever sits
here waiting, and who doesn't bleed down
from the chart though red flesh is showing.

He, too, like the x-ray is turned inside out,
and can't read the technical words on the margins
identifying his parts, or see the accompanying arrows
pointed at his organs as if he was a flayed saint
about to be pierced. Like you, he has been
here a long time, waiting and waiting,
and wants to climb down, slip
into skin, and walk out a complete man again.

Roadkill

Running over the dead
or the still breathing,
immobilized mid-road,
we stay with those animals
for miles even as we drive ahead.

They stick with us, too.
Once, after hitting an elk square,
already dead, with all tires
(no time to brake, swerve, pray)
I pulled into a final rest stop

on the edge of a dark city.
The tires, rims, lug nuts,
and chariot-style spokes
were still bleeding,
and those were the visible parts only.

That night, in a red darkness,
I dreamt of wheeling full circle
again and again.

Taps

For Erma

In her lap
she holds the dead,
her left hand, paralyzed,
like an unresponsive child.

She remembers its life.
Listening to live music
to which she must slap applause
against a table,
she rocks her wheelchair,
keeps time with the good hand
tapping on the other
as if to awaken the dead to play.

A Wheel in the Walk-In Clinic

Above our bowed heads
a TV game show is playing:
blanks turn to letters,
letters to words,
words to phrases.
The correct answers sit in the wings
like fat dictionaries.

A thin woman in front of me broadcasts a cough.
Now the contestants scream
and the audience hollers
as a wheel of fortune spins—
you know the game.

A pale man behind me
stares into nothing at my head.
Here in the walk-in clinic
the waiting list grows,
and no one speaks, no one looks up for long—
just a glance into a ceiling corner,
loud and colorful, where a sequined blonde
turns blanks, and the wheel spins again.

Presences

My mother slept with animals in the end,
a trained black Labrador
sauntering into her nursing home room,
or a registered collie,
both leaping into bed with her—
welcome, perpetual visitors
in our perpetual absence.
Once deemed "dirty" in our pet-free home,
before she was stricken, they now
curled around her dementia,
offered warm fur to touch
in lieu of missing hands,
and licked her stroke.

Birding
For my mother

We walk daily, hourly,
from the Memory Ward to an aviary,
from your dark room down
three white hallways, past residents
staring at nothing, at ghosts,
to a door whose code only I know.

I unlock the maze
that has locked you in.
We shuffle to a framed glass cage
crammed with color, flitting movements
on twigs, brief flights—finches
imported from Africa and South America,
their flamboyant captivity
capturing us.

We are silent;
in lieu of words,
muted songs.

Then we return to your wing,
repeat the ritual, return again
to the brightness of birds.

Tableau

In memory of my father

Seated so, a tight squeeze,
how do we talk over and around
your death bed? We can't,
and neither can you.
Only the numbers on the upright monitor
can speak, louder and louder,
in a precise language
no one can truly understand,
your tongue cut away by a stroke,
ours swallowed whole.

Last Dance

In the open-air building behind the VFW club,
an elderly couple two- steps beneath
ice tongs nailed to a cross beam
and under a flaking handsaw.
Other dancers circle below tractor pliers,
wooden pulleys, and washboards
wired to a plywood ceiling.

Farm antiques, precious rust,
hang like Damocles' swords.
An aging structure holds aloft
the weight of a lost world.

Yet no one looks up.
Arms circling, legs
swaying, feet sliding,
the old dance hand to hand,
eye to eye, to "The Midnight Special,"
then —more slowly—to "The Tennessee Waltz."

Winter Fields

All the corn stalks
and soybeans buried,
white contours
rise and fall,
flatten out,
and transform
as far as I can see.
You don't really know
the lay of the land
until it snows.

The Invisible

In memory of Carlos Morales,
former student of mime

He played a guitar that wasn't there,
but was there,
in his hands, in his movements,
swaying, eyes closed,
fingering strings composed of air.

He heard notes we could hear,
sad or joyous, though
they never made a sound.
He moved us as he moved,

and then he plucked from the gym floor
a flower and smelled it,
absorbing its essence to his roots,
and we realized that a flower
is more than a flower.

He sipped dark spirits
flowing down his throat,
pooling in his stomach,
the booze opening his eyes

wider and wider
until our eyes opened
and we tingled inside,
inebriated with amazement.

A balloon on a string
lifted him and us skyward.
Then we shivered in the rain
under his umbrella
full of holes.

He hoisted dumbbells,

staggered under their weight,
right, left, right,
our tense muscles
relaxing when he dropped iron.

For curtain call,
he pried open doors
to an elevator.
Alone, he entered,
pushed buttons,
stared at the floor numbers,

ascending or descending
in place, forty,
sixty, a hundred levels,
and stepped out into heaven
or hell, dazed, ecstatic,
anguished.

A year later,
a knife thrust into his heart,
lodged by a lover,
was one act he could not mime.

Acknowledgements

Without the inspiration, advice and encouragement from the following poets and writers, this book would not exist—David Coy, Ric Jahna, Portia Moore, and Rob Hardy, Poet Laureate of Northfield. I am also deeply appreciative of a Northfield poetry group, of which I am a contributing member, for all the invaluable suggestions, critical comments, and humor—David Walters, Becky Boling, D.E. Green, Heather Candels, and Julie Ryan. Thanks as well to Tom Driscoll for his indispensable help in publishing this book, and for publishing it in the first place. Finally, I must express an extra special thank you to my former English professor Emilio DeGrazia for his guidance, keen editorial skills, and brilliant insights.

About the Author

Steve McCown, a recently retired high school and parttime college teacher, graduated with a B.A. in English from Winona State University and with an M.A. in English from Northern Arizona University. After teaching in the deserts of southern California and Arizona for over 30 years, Steve returned to his native Minnesota, to Northfield, where he now resides with his wife Barbara and two semi-content cats.

Up On Big Rock Poetry Series
SHIPWRECKT BOOKS PUBLISHING COMPANY
Minnesota

Made in the USA
Columbia, SC
07 September 2020

18386344R00102